THE LITTLE BLACK BOOK OF
COCKTAILS

• *The Essential Guide to New & Old Classics* •

VIRGINIA REYNOLDS

ILLUSTRATED BY KERREN BARBAS

 PETER PAUPER PRESS, INC.
WHITE PLAINS, NEW YORK

PETER PAUPER PRESS
Fine Books and Gifts Since 1928

Our Company

In 1928, at the age of twenty-two, Peter Beilenson began printing books on a small press in the basement of his parents' home in Larchmont, New York. Peter—and later his wife, Edna—sought to create fine books that sold at "prices even a pauper could afford."

Today, still family owned and operated, Peter Pauper Press continues to honor our founders' legacy—and our customers' expectations—of beauty, quality, and value.

Thanks to Scott Levenson—my martini buddy—
and Ed Lieberthal, for the whiskey and the wisdom

Designed by Heather Zschock

Illustrations copyright © 2003
Kerren Barbas

Copyright © 2003
Peter Pauper Press, Inc.
202 Mamaroneck Avenue
White Plains, NY 10601
All rights reserved
ISBN 978-0-88088-360-3
Printed in Hong Kong

63 62 61 60 59 58

Visit us at www.peterpauper.com

Peter Pauper Press, Inc. and the author have used their best efforts to ensure that the ingredients and directions for each cocktail are correct. In addition, your attention is drawn to "How to Flame a Drink" on page 16 for correct handling of flaming cocktails. Nonetheless, we urge readers to use their discretion and good sense in making these cocktails, and not to do anything that seems ill advised. Finally, responsible drinking is everyone's personal responsibility.

THE LITTLE BLACK BOOK OF

COCKTAILS

CONTENTS

COCKTAIL CULTURE

COCKTAILS

The mere mention of the word conjures up an image of refinement, as it has during the 200-year history of cocktails. Today, the word cocktail refers to a mixed drink—usually spirits or liqueurs, sometimes prepared with a variety of fruit juices or carbonated mixers. Ironically, cocktails are traditionally served either before dinner—to make you hungrier—or after dinner, to make you more full.

The attendant rituals of cocktails call to mind the gentility of British colonials, the sophistication of the Jazz Age, and the smart, brash Rat Pack set of the 1950s and '60s.

What's your pleasure?

BEFORE YOU IMBIBE

A few pointers to enhance your drinking experience:

Your guests will forgive incorrect glassware sooner than they will poor quality liquor or badly mixed drinks. Use the best quality alcohol and mixers that you can afford. If your budget won't budge, invest in one type of liquor and throw a "gin" or "rum" party. Mix carefully. Drinks should be neither too strong nor too weak. Last, note your guests' preferences. Who enjoys a sweeter whiskey sour? Who likes lots of fizz or lime juice in a rum and coke?

Cocktails are always best served icy cold. Chill everything: your alcohol, mixers, glasses, and all mixing equipment. Glasses, especially, benefit from a few hours in the freezer.

Alcohol-only cocktails should be stirred, not shaken (sorry, 007). Drinks containing fruit juices should be shaken vigorously in a cocktail shaker or mixing glass. If you're adding a carbonated mixer, just finish with a quick stir from a cocktail spoon or swizzle stick.

Have plenty of cracked ice on hand. Always discard the ice in the cocktail shaker after mixing the drink. If the cocktail is to be served on the rocks, use fresh ice.

Mix drinks individually, on demand. Don't let a pitcher of Martinis or Manhattans stand around. The mixing and shaking of the cocktail is an integral part of the rite.

Don't refill glasses. Each cocktail deserves a clean, chilled glass.

Be sure to have non-alcoholic choices on hand, and encourage your guests to drink responsibly.

A full glossary of drinking terms and liquor descriptions can be found at the back of this book.

THE WELL-STOCKED BAR

You don't need flashy equipment. Nothing digital or electronic here—just a few implements that have been around since your grandparents were guzzling gin rickeys.

*A jigger measure—with half and quarter
  ounces clearly marked*
Mixing glass or metal cocktail shaker
Set of measuring spoons
Glass stirring rod or a long cocktail spoon
Bar strainer
Can opener, bottle opener, and corkscrew
Small sharp knife
Wooden muddler, or mortar and pestle
Ice bucket and tongs
Lemon/lime squeezer
Electric blender
Little bar towels

GLASSWARE

Champagne flute

Cocktail glass

Parfait glass

Highball glass

Old fashioned glass

Margarita glass

Punch cup

Pony glass

Short-stemmed oval glass

There's nothing more elegant than a long-stemmed cocktail glass. Holding the drink by the stem keeps your body heat away from the cocktail, resulting in a cocktail that stays colder longer. A cocktail glass holds 3-4 ounces.

In addition to these beauties—which are an absolute must—you'll need:

OLD FASHIONED GLASSES: *small tumblers for serving the drink of the same name and other on-the-rocks drinks. Also called "rocks glass"*
Capacity: 4 oz.

HIGHBALL GLASSES: *taller glasses for mixed highballs and other fizzy favorites*
Capacity: 8-10 oz.

PARFAIT GLASSES: *tulip-shaped goblets for frozen goodies*
Capacity: 12 oz.

CHAMPAGNE FLUTES: *Don't embarrass yourself by serving champagne in one of those wedding-style saucers.*
Capacity: 4-6 oz.

PONY OR POUSSE CAFÉ GLASSES: *shaped like champagne glasses, only smaller*
Capacity: 1 oz.

Optional, but always classy:

SHORT-STEMMED OVAL GLASSES: *ideal for whiskey sours and other sweet shorties* Capacity: 4 oz.

COLLINS GLASSES: *taller and slightly roomier than highball glasses* Capacity: 10-12 oz.

MARGARITA GLASSES: *saucer-shaped versions of a cocktail glass, and available in a variety of sizes*

PUNCH BOWL AND CUPS: *much more aesthetically appealing than serving your holiday punch in paper cups! Check garage sales for bargains.*

EDIBLE ACCESSORIES AND MIXERS

Accessories complete the outfit. They should match the main ingredient of the ensemble. You wouldn't pair blue shoes with a brown bag, would you? This is why you don't garnish a daiquiri with a cocktail onion.

Bearing in mind that many cocktails require

special or distinctive garnishes that you can purchase as needed, always keep the following essentials on hand:

FRUIT

Lemons	*Limes*
Maraschino cherries	*Oranges*
Olives	

SEASONINGS

Salt and pepper
Worcestershire sauce
Tabasco or other hot sauce

SWEET FLAVORINGS

Grenadine
Maraschino syrup

SIMPLE SYRUP

Many bartenders prefer simple syrup to sugar in sweetened cocktails because it blends easily and provides a smooth taste. They're right.

To make simple syrup:

Dissolve 1 pound granulated sugar in 8 ounces warm water. Stirring continually, add an additional 8 ounces water until sugar is completely dissolved. Store syrup in a jar with a tight-fitting lid.

MIXERS

Club soda or *soda water*—these are interchangeable.

Cola	*Pineapple juice*
Tonic water	*Tomato juice*
Ginger ale	*Cranberry juice*
Orange juice	

GARNISHING COCKTAILS

This sounds like a "learn to dance" video: the twist, the squeeze, the wheel.

THE TWIST

How to twist citrus peel:

Liberate those aromatic oils! Pare a section of fruit peel, taking care to take only the peel, not the bitter white pith. Rub the peel around the rim of the glass to deposit the essential oil. Twist gently until a drop or two of oil appears, and drop the peel into the glass.

THE SQUEEZE

The squeeze adds a little unadulterated juice and a slight bitterness that helps balance a drink's sweetness. A squeeze is a sixth or an eighth of a whole lemon or lime with both ends cut off. When serving a drink with a squeeze, cut a small slit into the fruit's side. Rest the fruit on the rim of the glass. Don't bother to squeeze—leave that pleasure to your guest.

THE WHEEL

Wheels are ideal garnishes for sweet drinks that require a slight afterbite of sharp flavor. Neatness counts here—use a sharp knife to make slices no wider than 1/4-inch.

HOW TO FLAME A DRINK

We're sure we don't need to say this, but the lawyer says we must: use extreme caution, and be sure to extinguish flames before drinking!

Warm glass and alcohol before you begin.

Prepare cocktail according to recipe.

Pour some of the highest proof alcohol into a spoon.

Ignite with a kitchen match or lighter.

Carefully pour flaming liquid into cocktail.

Serve immediately.

For a breathtaking sparkle effect, twist orange rind over the flame.

OCKTAILS CLASSIQUE

Standbys from the Age of Elegance

LIKE THE MUSIC OF COLE PORTER OR GERSHWIN, THESE STANDARDS REMIND US OF THE AGE OF SCOTT AND ZELDA, THE ALGONQUIN ROUND TABLE, SMOKE-FILLED DRAWING ROOMS AND SPARKLING WIT . . . AND LIKE PORTER AND FITZGERALD, THEIR ELEGANCE AND SOPHISTICATION WILL NEVER GO OUT OF FASHION.

AFFINITY COCKTAIL

1 oz. Scotch
3/4 oz. dry vermouth
3/4 oz. sweet vermouth
2-3 dashes orange bitters

Stir ingredients with cracked ice and strain into a chilled cocktail glass.

ALGONQUIN

2 oz. rye or blended whiskey
1 oz. dry vermouth
1 oz. pineapple juice

Stir ingredients with cracked ice and strain into a chilled cocktail glass. Garnish with a maraschino cherry.

AMERICAN BEAUTY

1/2 oz. brandy
1/2 oz. dry vermouth
1/4 teaspoon white crème de menthe
1/2 oz. grenadine
1/2 oz. fresh orange juice

Pour ingredients into a cocktail shaker and shake well with cracked ice. Strain into a chilled cocktail glass. Finish with a little port wine on top.

AMERICANO

1 oz. Campari
1/2 oz. sweet vermouth
Club soda

Stir first two ingredients in an iced rocks glass. Fill with club soda and garnish with an orange wheel.

AMER PICON COCKTAIL

Dash of grenadine
2 oz. Amer Picon
Juice of 1 lime

Coat the inside of a chilled cocktail glass with grenadine. Mix Amer Picon and lime juice in a cocktail shaker with cracked ice. Strain into cocktail glass. Alternatively, strain into an iced old fashioned glass and fill with soda water.

B & B

1/2 oz. Benedictine
1/2 oz. cognac

In a cordial glass, float cognac on top of the Benedictine. Pour cognac carefully down the side of the glass so that the ingredients do not mix.

BACARDI COCKTAIL

By law, this drink can be made only with Bacardi Rum. Really.

1-1/2 oz. Bacardi light rum
Juice of 1/2 fresh lime
Few drops of grenadine

Shake ingredients in a cocktail shaker with cracked ice. Strain into a chilled cocktail glass.

BELLINI

This delectable peach cocktail is enjoying a renaissance.

1-1/2 oz. peach juice (traditionally the juice of a fresh white *peach)*
Champagne

Pour peach juice or schnapps into a champagne flute. Fill glass with champagne and garnish with a fresh peach slice.

BLACK VELVET

1 oz. Guinness or other stout
3 oz. champagne

Pour Guinness carefully into a chilled champagne flute, taking care not to create too much foam. Slowly add champagne.

BLOODY MARY

Properly prepared, this spicy concoction can double as an hors d'oeuvre! *Adjust the seasonings to your taste. The addition of Tabasco sauce is a relatively recent, albeit tasty, innovation.*

1-1/2 oz. vodka
3 oz. tomato juice
1/2 oz. fresh lemon juice
Few drops of Worcestershire Sauce, to taste
Freshly ground black pepper
Dash of celery salt
Grated horseradish
Tabasco sauce

Pour ingredients into a cocktail shaker with cracked ice. Shake well and strain into an iced highball glass. Garnish with a lemon wedge and celery stick—leaves included.

For a VIRGIN MARY, omit vodka.

CHAMPAGNE COCKTAIL

Just because you're using the champagne in a cocktail recipe is no reason to stint on quality. You owe it to your guests to use good quality champagne.

Sugar cube
bitters
Champagne

Place a sugar cube in a chilled champagne flute and saturate with a few drops of bitters. Fill the glass with champagne.

FLAMINGO COCKTAIL

1-1/4 oz. gin
1/2 oz. apricot brandy
Dash of grenadine
Juice of 1/2 fresh lime

Mix with cracked ice and strain into a chilled cocktail glass.

HARRY'S BAR

Don't confuse Harry's in Venice with Harry's in Paris. Both are venerable institutions; both were beloved by Mr. Hemingway; and both remain popular with American expatriates, tourists, and literati.

HARRY'S BAR, PARIS

5 rue Daunou (2nd Arrondissement)—just remember "sank roo doe noo."

- Opened 1911 by American expatriate Harry MacElhone.

- Quickly became the neighborhood pub to many Jazz Age legends, including William Faulkner, Henry Miller, and Sinclair Lewis.

- Creators of the **BLOODY MARY**, **FRENCH 75**, and possibly the **SIDECAR**, among others.

HARRY'S BAR, VENICE

On the St. Mark's Bay waterfront.

- Opened in 1931 by the Cipriani family, which still owns and operates it.

- Creators of the BELLINI cocktail and beef carpaccio.

- Favored by an assortment of glitterati, including the Aga Khan, Truman Capote, and Orson Welles.

FRENCH 75

For a Champagne Collins, substitute gin for cognac.

1-1/2 oz. cognac
4 oz. dry champagne
1/2 oz. simple syrup
1 oz. fresh lemon juice

Dissolve syrup in lemon juice in an iced highball glass. Add cognac and fill with champagne. Stir very gently.

GIMLET

2-1/4 oz. gin or vodka
3/4 oz. Rose's Lime Juice

Stir with cracked ice and strain into a chilled cocktail glass. A dash of bitters will color this drink a pleasant shade of pink.

GIN AND IT

Traditionally, no ice was used in this drink. However, it can be served like its cousin, the martini, in a chilled cocktail glass and no one will be the wiser.

1-1/2 oz. gin
1-1/2 oz. sweet vermouth

Stir with cracked ice and strain into a cocktail glass. Add a dash of bitters, if desired, and garnish with a twist of orange peel.

GIN RICKEY

1-1/2 oz. gin
Juice of 1/2 fresh lime
Soda water

Add gin and lime to iced highball glass. Fill glass with soda water and garnish with a lime wedge.

HIGHBALLS

Highballs are refreshing, easy to prepare, and lend themselves to endless variations. They are always served on the rocks. Combine 1-1/2 ounces of your choice of alcohol in an iced highball glass with any carbonated mixer: club soda, ginger ale, lemon-lime soda, or cola.

A FEW OF THE ALL-TIME FAVORITES:

GIN BUCK

Gin and ginger ale, with a dash of fresh lemon juice. Garnish with a lemon wedge.

GIN 'N TONIC

Gin and tonic water. Garnish with a lime wedge. Always popular among British colonials in tropical climes, as the quinine in tonic water was believed to help prevent malaria.

HORSE'S NECK
Blended whiskey and ginger ale, garnished with a twist of lemon peel.

RUM & COKE
Garnish with a lime wedge and a tropical breeze.

SCOTCH & SODA
Always, always with a twist of lemon peel.

7 & 7
Seagram's 7 Crown blended whiskey and 7-Up soda.

STONE FENCE
Scotch whisky, club soda, and a dash of bitters.

HIGHLAND COOLER

1/2 tsp. sugar
2 oz. scotch

In an iced highball glass, dissolve sugar in some soda water or ginger ale. Add scotch and fill up with mixer. Garnish with a twist of orange peel.

KIR ROYALE

1/2 oz. Crème de Cassis
Champagne

Pour Crème de Cassis into a chilled champagne flute and fill with champagne.

MANHATTAN

This classic was created at the Manhattan Club in New York City during a party thrown by Lady Randolph Churchill in honor of New York mayor Samuel J. Tilden.

1-1/2 oz. blended whiskey
3/4 oz. sweet vermouth
Dash of bitters

Stir with cracked ice and strain into a chilled cocktail glass or on the rocks. Garnish with a maraschino cherry.

PERFECT MANHATTAN

A Manhattan, but use equal parts of sweet and dry vermouth and garnish with a twist of lemon peel.

MIMOSA

Champagne
Freshly squeezed orange juice (no seeds,
* please!)*
Dash of Grand Marnier

Use more champagne than orange juice, to
taste. Serve in a champagne flute.

NEGRONI

During the 1930s, Count Camilo Negroni
enjoyed his Americano cocktails with a little
something extra. Instead of soda water, he
would add gin. . . and the rest is cocktail his-
tory. If it's fizz you're after, add soda water.

1-1/2 oz. gin
1-1/2 oz. Campari
1-1/2 oz. sweet vermouth

Stir ingredients with ice and strain into
chilled cocktail glass.

NEW YORK COCKTAIL

1-1/2 oz. blended whiskey
1 tsp. simple syrup
Few dashes of grenadine
Juice of 1 lime

Shake well with cracked ice and strain into an iced old fashioned glass. Garnish with a twist of lemon or orange peel.

OLD FASHIONED

Kentucky bourbon distiller James E. Pepper invented this cocktail during the late 19th century in the bar of the Pendennis Club in Louisville.

2 oz. bourbon or blended whiskey
Splash of simple syrup
2 dashes bitters

Add ingredients to iced rocks glass and garnish with a cherry.

As a variation, add 1 ounce club soda for fizz. Or muddle an orange slice and a cherry in the bottom of the glass before adding other ingredients, and garnish with another orange slice and cherry.

ORANGE BLOSSOM

2 oz. gin
1 oz. orange juice
1/4 tsp. sugar

Stir with cracked ice and strain into a chilled cocktail glass. Garnish with orange slice.

PINK GIN

2 oz. gin
Dash of bitters

Swirl a dash of bitters in a cocktail glass until the inside of the glass is completely coated. Fill glass with gin. A cube of cracked ice and/or a twist of lemon peel may be added.

ROB ROY

This variation of the Manhattan cocktail is named for the legendary 17th century Scottish brigand Robert MacGregor.

1-1/2 oz. Scotch
3/4 oz. sweet vermouth
Dash of bitters

Serve over ice in a rocks glass, or shake with cracked ice and strain into a chilled cocktail glass. Garnish with a cherry.

For a **PERFECT ROB ROY**, use equal parts dry and sweet vermouth. Using all dry vermouth will produce a dry version. Either should be garnished with a twist of lemon peel.

RUSTY NAIL

1-1/2 oz. Scotch
1 oz. Drambuie

Serve on the rocks.

SAZERAC COCKTAIL

During the 19th century, rye whiskey replaced French Sazerac brandy, and Pernod now replaces absinthe in this New Orleans classic. Prepare this drink in as cold a glass as possible.

2 oz. rye whiskey
1/4 tsp. Pernod or other anise-flavored
    liqueur
1/2 tsp. sugar
Few dashes Peychaud's bitters (accept NO
    substitutes)

Swirl some Pernod in an icy cold old fashioned glass until the sides of the glass are completely coated. Pour out excess. Pour sugar and bitters into a cocktail shaker with cracked ice and shake very well. Add rye. Strain into an old fashioned glass, and add a long twist of lemon peel (twist and squeeze gently before dropping the peel into the glass).

THE NAPOLEON HOUSE

*"The interior of Napoleon House was dark
and inviting, kept deliberately in a state of
careful decay, with faded paintings of the
emperor on the walls. Beethoven's Eroica
enveloped the room, the only music allowed
here that wasn't opera. . . . The place was
perfect."* —ANDREI CODRESCU, *MESSIAH*

Splendidly decadent, The Napoleon House
is a landmark in New Orleans' French
Quarter. Its original occupant, Nicholas
Girod—New Orleans mayor from 1812 to
1815—offered his residence to the exiled
Emperor Napoleon. Although Napoleon
declined the offer, the name stuck.

In a city renowned for jazz, the Napoleon

House offers the unexpected: classical music and quirky cocktails. Enjoy a Sazerac Cocktail or Pimm's Cup in the courtyard with a dash of dissipation.

SCOTCH MIST

2 oz. scotch
Crushed ice

Pour scotch whisky over crushed ice in an old fashioned glass. Add a generous twist of lemon peel. This drink is often served with two short, thin straws.

SCREWDRIVER

2 oz. vodka
Freshly squeezed orange juice (no seeds,
*   please)*

Pour vodka into an iced highball glass and fill with orange juice. Garnish with an orange slice.

SIDECAR

Which Paris watering hole can claim this WWI gem? Harry's? The Ritz? Legend has it that an officer arrived at his favorite bar one evening chilled to the bone from his motorcycle trip and requested a warming drink. Whatever the origins of this celebrated cocktail, it became an instant classic and remains popular today.

1-1/2 oz. cognac or brandy
3/4 oz. Cointreau (do not be tempted to substitute triple sec)
Juice of 1/4 lemon

Mix in cocktail shaker with cracked ice and strain into a chilled cocktail glass.

SINGAPORE SLING

Created in that bastion of British colonial elegance, Raffles Hotel, Singapore, this cocktail boasts an impressive pedigree dating back to the 1880s.

1-1/2 oz. gin
1/2 oz. cherry brandy or Cherry Heering
Few drops Benedictine
Juice of 1/2 lemon
Soda water

Mix in cocktail shaker with cracked ice and strain into an iced highball glass. Fill with soda water and garnish with a lemon slice. If desired, sweeten with a little simple syrup.

SLOE GIN FIZZ

Technically a Collins, this drink is so famous that we had to give it its own entry.

2 oz. sloe gin
1/2 oz. fresh lemon juice
1 tsp. simple syrup
Soda water

Shake all ingredients well in a cocktail shaker and strain into an iced highball glass. Fill to the top with soda water. Garnish with a lemon slice.

STINGER

2 oz. brandy
3/4 oz. white crème de menthe

Mix in cocktail shaker with cracked ice and strain into a chilled cocktail glass. May also be served on the rocks in an old fashioned glass.

TOM COLLINS

This refreshing group of drinks has a family tree that dates back to the early 19th century. Always serve a Collins drink in a frosty highball glass with lots of cracked ice.

2 oz. gin
1 tsp. sugar
Juice of 1/2 fresh lemon
Soda water

Place sugar and lemon juice in an iced highball glass. Add gin and fill with soda water. Stir with a swizzle stick and garnish with a lemon wedge and cherry.

CRANBERRY COLLINS

1-1/2 oz. gin
1/2 oz. cranberry juice
Juice of a fresh lime
Club soda

Place all ingredients in an iced highball glass. Fill with club soda. Stir with a swizzle stick and garnish with a lime wedge.

JOHN COLLINS

Substitute bourbon for gin.

PEDRO COLLINS

Substitute light rum for gin.

SANDY COLLINS

Substitute scotch for gin.

VODKA COLLINS

Substitute vodka for gin.

WARD EIGHT

1-1/2 oz. blended whiskey
1 tsp. simple syrup
Juice of 1/2 fresh lemon
1 tsp. grenadine

Shake all ingredients well in a cocktail shaker with cracked ice. Strain into a chilled cocktail glass and garnish with a skewer of orange, lemon, and a cherry.

WHISKEY SOUR

One simple rule: throw away your packaged sour mix and avail yourself of fresh lemons. It is worth the effort.

2 oz. blended whiskey
1/2 oz. simple syrup
Juice of 1/2 fresh lemon

Shake all ingredients well in a cocktail shaker with cracked ice. Strain into a chilled cocktail glass and garnish with an orange slice and a cherry.

Substitute brandy, gin, rum, or flavored liqueurs for the whiskey to create variations.

THE MARTINI

Introducing the Grand Duke of Cocktails

SO IMPORTANT, WE HAD TO GIVE IT ITS OWN CHAPTER

Nothing matches the mystique of the martini. It's the ultimate cocktail for cool cats and lounge lizards alike.

The classic martini is made with gin and vermouth. Although nowadays martinis are often made with vodka, purists still insist on gin. The "dryness" of the martini depends on the amount of vermouth used; less vermouth results in a "drier" martini. Back in the swanky 1960s, people were accustomed to a lower ratio of gin to vermouth, sometimes a 1:1 ratio. The modern trend is for drier martinis—often an 8:1 ratio. Experimentation will help you discover your own "perfect martini."

In the recipes below, vodka may sometimes be substituted for gin. However, be careful not to substitute gin where vodka is specified, as gin imparts a distinctive flavor to the drink, which—as in the case of the Mango Martini or other flavored martinis—may be undesirable.

All components should be cold—bitterly cold. If at all convenient, store both the alcohol and glasses in the freezer.

CLASSIC MARTINI

1-1/2 oz. gin (or vodka)
1/2 oz. dry vermouth

Using a teaspoon or, ideally, a glass cocktail stirrer, stir with ice cubes—never crushed ice—and strain into a chilled cocktail glass. Garnish with a twist of lemon peel or an olive.

DRY MARTINI

2-1/2 oz. gin
1/3 oz. dry vermouth

EXTRA DRY MARTINI

2-3/4 oz. gin
1/4 oz. dry vermouth

For a BUCKEYE MARTINI, use a black olive. For a GIBSON, use a pickled cocktail onion. Add up to a quarter-ounce of single malt Scotch whisky, and you have a SMOKY MARTINI. For a DIRTY MARTINI, add a splash of olive brine.

MEDIUM MARTINI

2 oz. gin
1 oz. dry vermouth, or half dry, half sweet
vermouth

SWEET MARTINI

2 oz. gin
3/4 oz. sweet vermouth

WET MARTINI

1-1/2 oz. gin
1-1/2 oz. dry vermouth

*Martinis should always be stirred,
not shaken, so that the molecules lie
sensuously on top of one another.*

SOMERSET MAUGHAM

MARTINI MADNESS

*Try these chic variations on the classic, or invent
your own! Flavored vodkas—orange, vanilla,
even hot pepper—make for endless possibilities.*

APPLE MARTINI

*1-1/2 oz. vodka (regular or apple flavored)
1/2 oz. apple liqueur
Splash of lemon juice*

Stir with cracked ice and strain into a chilled
cocktail glass. Garnish with an apple slice or
apple candy.

BLUE VELVET MARTINI

1-1/2 oz. vodka
1/4 oz. blue Curaçao
Dash of Rose's lime juice

Stir with cracked ice and strain into a chilled cocktail glass. Garnish with a slice of lemon.

CAJUN MARTINI

1-1/2 oz. gin or hot pepper-flavored vodka
1/2 oz. vermouth
Dash hot sauce

Stir with cracked ice and strain into a chilled cocktail glass. Garnish with a pickled jalapeño pepper (but don't eat it!).

CHOCOLATE MARTINI

1-1/2 oz. vodka (regular or vanilla flavored)
1/2 oz. dark chocolate liqueur
1/2 oz. white chocolate liqueur

Stir with cracked ice and strain into a chilled cocktail glass. Garnish with shavings of bittersweet chocolate.

CRANTINI

1-1/2 oz. vodka
2 oz. cranberry juice
Juice of 1/4 fresh lime

Stir with cracked ice and strain into a chilled cocktail glass. Garnish with a lime wheel.

EMERALD MARTINI

1-1/2 oz. gin
1/2 oz. dry vermouth
1/8 oz. Chartreuse liqueur

Stir with cracked ice and strain into a chilled cocktail glass. Garnish with a twist of lemon or lime peel.

ESPRESSO MARTINI

1-1/2 oz. vodka (regular or vanilla flavored)
1/2 oz. Crème de Cacao

Stir with cracked ice and strain into a chilled cocktail glass. Garnish with 2 or 3 espresso beans.

GOLDENEYE MARTINI

Another contribution from the world of 007

2 oz. vodka
Few drops of Black Sambuca

Moisten the rim of a chilled cocktail glass with the juice of a fresh lime. Spin glass rim in sugar. Stir vodka and Sambuca with cracked ice and strain into glass. Garnish with a lime wheel.

MANGO MARTINI

1-1/2 oz. vodka
1 oz. unsweetened mango juice

Stir with cracked ice; strain into a chilled cocktail glass. Garnish with a slice of mango.

MARTINEZ

3/4 oz. gin
3/4 oz. dry vermouth
1/2 oz. Cointreau
Dash of bitters

Stir with cracked ice and strain into a chilled cocktail glass. Garnish with a maraschino cherry or a slice of lemon.

MARTINI ROYALE

2 oz. gin
Champagne

Pour chilled gin into a chilled cocktail glass.
Top with champagne, and garnish with a
twist of lemon peel.

MÉDOC MARTINI

2 oz. gin
1/2 oz. Cordial Médoc
Dash of dry vermouth

Stir with cracked ice and strain into a chilled
cocktail glass. Garnish with a twist of lemon
peel.

MIDNIGHT MARTINI

1-1/2 oz. vodka
1/4 oz. coffee liqueur
1/4 oz. triple sec or orange liqueur

Stir with cracked ice and strain into a chilled cocktail glass. Garnish with an orange slice.

MINT MARTINI

1-1/2 oz. vodka
1 oz. peppermint schnapps or liqueur

Stir with cracked ice and strain into a chilled cocktail glass. Garnish with a peppermint stick or sprig of fresh mint. Perfect for the holidays!

NUTTY MARTINI

2-1/2 oz. vodka
1/2 oz. Frangelico

Stir with cracked ice and strain into a chilled

cocktail glass. Garnish with a twist of orange peel.

PINEAPPLE FLIRTINI

1-1/2 oz. vodka
1-1/2 oz. champagne
Splash of pineapple juice

Stir with cracked ice and strain into a chilled cocktail glass. Garnish with a pineapple slice.

PRINCESS MARTINI

1-1/2 oz. vodka
Splash of strawberry liqueur

Stir with cracked ice and strain into a chilled cocktail glass. Garnish with a twist of orange peel.

RUBY MARTINI

1-1/2 oz. vodka
1/2 oz. cranberry juice
1/2 oz. blue Curaçao

Stir with cracked ice and strain into a chilled cocktail glass.

SAKETINI

1-1/2 oz. gin
1/4 oz. sake

Stir with cracked ice and strain into a chilled cocktail glass. Garnish with a slice of fresh cucumber.

SAPPHIRE MARTINI

*1-1/2 oz. Bombay Sapphire Gin (renowned
for its spicy flavor)*
1/2 oz. blue Curaçao liqueur

Stir with cracked ice and strain into a chilled
cocktail glass. Garnish with chilled blueberries or crystallized violets.

TEQUINI

1-1/2 oz. tequila
1/2 oz. dry vermouth

Shake with ice and serve on the rocks, or
strain into a chilled cocktail glass. Garnish
with a slice of lime or twist of lime peel.

VESPER

The martini made famous in Ian Fleming's Casino Royale and beloved of James Bond aficionados the world over. Remember, despite Somerset Maugham's entreaties, Bond believes that "shaken, not stirred" is the key to avoiding "bruising the gin."

1-1/2 oz. gin
1/2 oz. vodka
1/3 oz. Lillet

Add ingredients to an ice-filled cocktail shaker and shake well. Strain into a chilled cocktail glass and garnish with a generous twist of lemon peel.

URBAN CHIC

The Next Generation—Sophisticated and Modern

COCKTAILS HAVE EVOLVED CONSIDERABLY OVER
THE PAST 50 YEARS. THE COCKTAIL SHAKERS OF
TODAY ARE SHAKING OUT FRESH NEW TASTES—
SOME FRUITY, SOME POTENT, SOME SWEET—
WORTHY HEIRS OF THE GOLDEN AGE.

ALABAMA SLAMMER

1 oz. Southern Comfort
1 oz. Amaretto
1/2 oz. sloe gin
Dash of fresh lemon juice

Mix in cocktail shaker with cracked ice and strain into an iced highball glass. Garnish with a cherry or lemon slice.

BLIZZARD

1-1/2 oz. blended whiskey
2 tsp. simple syrup
1 oz. cranberry juice
Juice of 1/4 fresh lemon

Mix in cocktail shaker with cracked ice and strain into an iced highball glass. Garnish with a lemon slice.

BOHEMIAN

2 oz. vodka
1 oz. pineapple juice
1/2 oz. passion fruit juice
1/2 oz. cranberry juice (or Aronia berry juice,
  if available)

Mix with cracked ice and strain into a chilled cocktail glass. Garnish with a red raspberry.

CAESAR

Bored with Bloody Marys? Here's a new twist on an old favorite.

1 oz. vodka
4 oz. Clamato juice
Salt and pepper to taste
Dash Worcestershire sauce
Horseradish
Celery salt

Moisten the rim of a chilled highball glass

and coat with celery salt. Stir other ingredients in a cocktail shaker with cracked ice. Strain into salted glass and adjust seasonings to taste. Garnish with a celery stalk and a lemon wedge.

CAIPIRINHA

A recent immigrant from Brazil, the Caipirinha is prepared with cachaça, a potent spirit distilled from sugar cane.

2 oz. cachaça
1 oz. simple syrup
1/2 lime, quartered

Place lime in a chilled old fashioned glass and muddle with simple syrup until lime is mushy. Add cachaça and cracked ice and mix well.

No cachaça where you live? Substitute vodka for cachaça, and you will have a CAIPIROSKA. Substitute light rum for cachaça for a CAIPIRÍSSIMA.

CAPE CODDER

2 oz. vodka
4-6 oz. cranberry juice

Mix in cocktail shaker with cracked ice and strain into an iced highball glass. If desired, add a dash of fresh lime juice and garnish with a lime wedge.

COSMOPOLITAN

If you watch Sex and the City, *you're familiar with the snazzy Cosmopolitan, which clearly lives up to its name!*

2 oz. vodka
2 oz. cranberry juice
1 oz. fresh lime juice
3/4 oz. Cointreau

Stir with cracked ice and strain into a chilled cocktail glass. Garnish with a lime wedge.

THE ALGONQUIN HOTEL

A group of New York writers, critics, and theater personalities met almost daily in the Rose Room of the Algonquin Hotel throughout the 1920s. Such luminaries as Edna Ferber, Franklin P. Adams, Robert Sherwood, and Dorothy Parker traded witticisms and became known as the Algonquin Round Table—although they referred to themselves as "The Vicious Circle."

One more drink, and I'll be under the host.

DOROTHY PARKER

DELILAH

2 oz. gin
1 oz. Cointreau
1 oz. fresh lemon juice

Stir with cracked ice and strain into a chilled cocktail glass.

FUZZY NAVEL

2 oz. peach schnapps
4 oz. fresh orange juice

Mix in cocktail shaker with cracked ice and strain into an iced highball glass. Garnish with orange or peach slice.

HAIRY NAVEL

Add 1 ounce vodka and mix as above.

GODFATHER

1 oz. scotch
1 oz. Amaretto

Mix in cocktail shaker with cracked ice and strain into an iced old fashioned glass.

Substitute vodka for scotch, and presto: a GODMOTHER.

HARVEY WALLBANGER

2 oz. vodka
6 oz. fresh orange juice
Float of Galliano

Mix vodka and orange juice in cocktail shaker with cracked ice and strain into an iced highball glass. Float Galliano on top.

LEAP YEAR

Perfect for February 29th, but may be drunk on other days.

1-1/2 oz. gin
1/2 oz. sweet vermouth
1/2 oz. Grand Marnier
Few drops of fresh lemon juice

Stir with cracked ice and strain into a chilled cocktail glass.

LEMON DROP

1-1/2 oz. lemon-flavored vodka
3/4 oz. fresh lemon juice
1 tsp. simple syrup

Stir with cracked ice and strain into a chilled cocktail glass.

You may omit simple syrup and lemon juice, and serve with a sugared lemon wedge.

LONG ISLAND ICED TEA

Oh, the controversy! Oh, the variations! After extensive research, the editors tipsily agree that the recipe below captures the elusive essence of this potent cooler.

3/4 oz. rum
3/4 oz. gin
3/4 oz. vodka
3/4 oz. tequila
3/4 oz. triple sec
1 oz. fresh lemon juice
Cola

Mix all ingredients in a cocktail shaker and strain into an iced highball glass. Top with cola and garnish with a generous lemon wedge.

MATADOR

2 oz. tequila
1 oz. lime juice
4 oz. pineapple juice
2 tsp. simple syrup

Mix ingredients in blender and blend until slushy. Serve over ice cubes in a tall glass garnished with a lime wedge and pineapple chunk.

METROPOLITAN

1-1/4 oz. brandy
1-1/4 oz. sweet vermouth
1/2 tsp. simple syrup
Dash of bitters

Stir with cracked ice and strain into a chilled cocktail glass.

MIND ERASER

1-1/2 oz. vodka
1-1/2 oz. Kahlúa
Soda water

Pour Kahlúa into an iced old fashioned glass. Add vodka slowly to create a float. Fill with soda water, but don't mix. Serve with a straw.

NEW FASHION

2 oz. lemon flavored vodka
1/4 oz. sweet vermouth
1 tsp. simple syrup
3/4 oz. fresh lemon juice

Muddle an orange slice with simple syrup and lemon juice in the bottom of an iced old-fashioned glass. Mix other ingredients in a cocktail shaker with cracked ice and strain into the muddled orange mixture. Garnish with an orange wheel.

PEGU CLUB COCKTAIL

Named for the Pegu Club, formerly located near Rangoon. Deserves a comeback, which is why we've added it to this section.

1-1/2 oz. gin
3/4 oz. Curaçao or Cointreau
1 tsp. fresh lime juice
2 dashes of bitters

Stir with cracked ice and strain into a chilled cocktail glass.

PETIT ZINC

1 oz. vodka
1/2 oz. Cointreau
1/2 oz. sweet vermouth
1/2 oz. fresh orange juice (preferably from Seville oranges)

Stir with cracked ice and strain into a chilled cocktail glass. Garnish with a cherry or orange slice.

PURPLE HAZE

1 oz. vodka
1 oz. blue Curaçao
Cranberry juice

Mix vodka and blue Curaçao in a cocktail shaker and strain into an iced highball glass. Fill with cranberry juice and garnish with a cherry.

SALTY DOG

1-1/2 oz. vodka (or gin, if you prefer)
6 oz. fresh grapefruit juice

Mix ingredients in a cocktail shaker. Dust the rim of a chilled highball glass with salt. Add cracked ice and strain shaken ingredients into the glass.

SEA BREEZE

1-1/2 oz. vodka
2 oz. cranberry juice
2 oz. grapefruit juice

Mix all ingredients in a cocktail shaker and strain into an iced highball glass.

SILVER BULLET

1-1/2 oz. gin
1 oz. kümmel
1/2 oz. fresh lemon juice

Mix with cracked ice and strain into a chilled cocktail glass.

TEQUILA SUNRISE

1-1/2 oz. tequila
6 oz. fresh orange juice
1/2 oz. grenadine

Pour tequila and orange juice into an iced highball glass and float grenadine on top.

WILD BLUE YONDER

1-1/2 oz. vodka
1/4 oz. peach schnapps
1/4 oz. blue Curaçao

Mix ingredients with cracked ice in a cocktail shaker. Strain into a chilled cocktail glass or serve on the rocks.

PUNCH UP THAT PARTY!

Holiday cheer, seasonal favorites, and other potent potables

PUNCH HAS BEEN A PARTY PLEASER FOR DECADES.
IT FREES YOU (THE HOST) FROM ENDLESS TOIL
BEHIND THE BAR AND ENABLES YOU TO PARTY
ALONGSIDE YOUR GUESTS.

Cold punches—perfect for outdoor summer gatherings—usually contain citrus juices, spirits, and/or wine. Spice up your next holiday party with a simmering hot punch fragrant with wine and cinnamon.

PUNCH POINTERS:

- Budget about 2 five-ounce servings per guest.

- Serve a hot punch in a slow cooker or tureen.

- Make sure beforehand that your punch cups can tolerate a hot beverage. Or, serve hot punch in mugs.

- Warm punch cups or mugs in a hot water bath.

- Freeze cold punch ingredients (except carbonated mixers) for several hours before preparing punch.

- Never use ice cubes in a punch—they'll melt too fast. Freeze fruit juice into a block or in a gelatin mold and place in the punch bowl.

- Consider making several small batches of punch instead of one large batch. The punch will stay colder, and fizzy ingredients will stay fizzy longer.

- Prepare a non-alcoholic version of your punch for non-imbibing guests.

- Although it's not necessary to use top-shelf liquor in your punch, you should use something you wouldn't be ashamed to drink in an ordinary cocktail.

- Add fizzy ingredients last.

APRICOT BUBBLES PUNCH

1 large can (46 oz.) apricot nectar
12 oz. frozen orange juice concentrate
6 oz. frozen lemon juice concentrate
   (unsweetened)
18 oz. pineapple juice
1 bottle (750 ml.) white wine, preferably
   Sauterne
1 bottle (750 ml.) light rum
2 bottles (2 liters each) lemon/lime soda

Allow frozen juices to thaw; then mix all ingredients with ice in punch bowl. Add soda just before serving. Decorate with fruit slices, cherries, and strawberries.

40 5-OUNCE SERVINGS

BOMBAY PUNCH

3 oz. maraschino syrup or grenadine

3 oz. apricot liqueur

3 oz. Curaçao or Cointreau

2 cups sherry

2 cups brandy

1 liter soda water

*1 liter ginger ale, or 1/2 liter ginger ale plus
    1/2 liter champagne*

Pour all ingredients except fizzies into a punch bowl with a large block of ice. Add fizzies just before serving. Garnish with slices of fresh fruit and sprigs of sugared mint.

25 5-OUNCE SERVINGS

BUCKS FIZZ

No brunch party would be complete without this popular relative of the patrician Mimosa.

Use 3 parts champagne to 1 part orange juice, and stir very gently. Mix individually in chilled highball glasses.

CITRUS SPARKLER PUNCH

25 oz. gin

6 oz. frozen orange juice concentrate

12 oz. frozen lemonade or limeade concentrate (or 6 oz. of each)

6 oz. frozen pineapple/grapefruit juice concentrate

3 oz. fresh lime juice (if using limeade only, substitute 3 oz. unsweetened grapefruit juice)

2 liters soda water

Pour all ingredients except soda water into a punch bowl with a large block of ice. Add soda water just before serving. Garnish with lemon, lime, and orange slices.

24 5-OUNCE SERVINGS

CHAMPAGNE PUNCH

4 oz. fresh lemon juice
4 oz. unsweetened pineapple juice
3 oz. grenadine or maraschino syrup
1 cup brandy
3 oz. triple sec or Cointreau
1 (750 ml.) bottle white wine
2 bottles (750 ml. each) chilled champagne

Pour all ingredients except champagne over ice and stir. Add champagne just before serving. Garnish with fruit slices and fresh strawberries. For a less potent punch, substitute one liter of soda water or ginger ale for 1 bottle of champagne.

20 5-OUNCE SERVINGS

EGG NOG

Due to the health risks associated with raw eggs, we suggest using pasteurized eggs or egg substitutes in any recipe calling for raw eggs. Do not let these concerns deter you from enjoying this delicious seasonal treat, however.

12 eggs, separated
1 cup sugar
1 quart heavy cream
1 quart milk
1 quart blended whiskey or bourbon
1 cup rum or brandy

Beat egg yolks with sugar until sugar dissolves. Add cream, milk, and liquor, then stiffly beaten egg whites. Chill for several hours and sprinkle with grated nutmeg.

30-40 SERVINGS

FISH HOUSE PUNCH

A true American original, Fish House Punch was first prepared in Philadelphia in 1732, and is reported to have been a favorite of George Washington.

6 oz. simple syrup
24 oz. fresh lemon juice
1 bottle (750 ml.) light rum
1 bottle (750 ml.) dark rum
1 bottle (750 ml.) brandy
8 oz. peach brandy or liqueur
2 liters soda water

Pour all ingredients over a block of ice, adding soda water last. Garnish with fruit slices and mint leaves.

30 5-OUNCE SERVINGS

HOT SPICED CRANBERRY PUNCH

3/4 cup firmly packed brown sugar
1/4 tsp. salt
1/4 tsp. grated nutmeg
1/2 tsp. ground cinnamon
1/2 tsp. ground allspice
3/4 tsp. ground cloves
2 cans jellied cranberry sauce
4 cups pineapple juice
2 cups light rum

Bring to a boil sugar, 1 cup water, salt, and spices. Mash cranberry sauce with a fork. Add 3 cups water to cranberry sauce and beat with rotary beater until smooth. Add cranberry liquid and pineapple juice to hot spiced syrup and heat to boiling. Add rum. Serve hot with cinnamon stick stirrers.

20 5-OUNCE SERVINGS

MULLED WINE

In merrie olde England, revelers would heat a fireplace poker and thrust it into the punch bowl. Do not try this at home.

Peel of 1/2 lemon, cut into curls
Peel of 1/2 orange, cut into curls
2 Tbs. sugar
1 tsp. ground allspice
2 tsp. ground cinnamon
2 tsp. ground cloves
3 cups boiling water
2 bottles full-bodied red wine

Pour boiling water over the fruit peel, sugar, and spices and simmer for 10 minutes. Place in a punch bowl. Heat wine to just below the boiling point, and add. Add rum. Dot with butter and serve with cinnamon stick stirrers.

18 5-OUNCE SERVINGS

PLANTER'S PUNCH

Traditionally prepared individually in an iced highball glass, this standard still packs a punch!

2 oz. light rum
2 tsp. simple syrup
Juice of 2 fresh limes
1 oz. dark rum
Soda water
Few drops of bitters

Pour light rum, syrup, and lime juice into a highball glass filled with crushed ice and stir until glass is frosted. Add dark rum. Fill with soda water and top with bitters. Garnish with fresh fruit and sugared mint sprigs.

1 SERVING

RED VELVET PUNCH

8 cups cranberry juice
1 cup fresh cranberries
2 cups brandy
2 bottles (750 ml. each) champagne
6 oz. frozen orange juice concentrate
6 oz. frozen pineapple juice concentrate
6 oz. frozen lemon juice concentrate

Freeze 2 cups of cranberry juice into a block with fresh cranberries. Allow frozen juices to thaw. Mix all ingredients except champagne in punch bowl over cranberry ice. Add champagne just before serving. Garnish with fruit slices.

24 5-OUNCE SERVINGS

RUM PUNCH

6 lemons, juiced and grated
6 oz. sugar
2 tsp. ground ginger
1 bottle (750 ml.) golden rum
1 bottle (750 ml.) brandy
1 cup sherry
1-1/2 quarts boiling water

Mix and muddle lemon juice and gratings, sugar, and ginger. Let stand for at least 1 hour. Place in a large bowl and add enough hot water to cover. Stir thoroughly and add liquors and balance of hot water.

12 5-OUNCE SERVINGS

SANGRÍA

1 bottle (750 ml.) full-bodied red wine
2 oz. brandy
2 oz. simple syrup
Sliced oranges and lemons
1 cup soda water

Stir ingredients in a pitcher with ice cubes made from red wine and/or orange juice. Add soda water just before serving. For additional sweetness, substitute ginger ale or lemon/lime soda for soda water.

8-10 SERVINGS

YULETIDE WASSAIL

Traditionally, one is supposed to sing a song before partaking of the communal wassailing bowl. Your hosts may wish to dispense with this convention—then again, maybe they won't.

1 quart ale
1 quart brandy or light rum, warmed slightly

1/4 tsp. grated nutmeg
1/4 tsp. ground ginger
Grated peel of 1 lemon
3 eggs
4 oz. sugar

Heat ale almost to the boiling point with nutmeg, ginger, and lemon peel. Beat eggs with sugar. Add a little hot ale to the egg mixture to equalize the temperature and keep the eggs from scrambling. Gradually add egg mixture to the hot ale. Pour mixture into a pitcher. Pour warmed brandy into another pitcher. Turn ingredients from one pitcher into the other until mixture is smooth. Pour into your vessel of choice—traditionally a holly-wreathed Wassailing Bowl. Do not eat holly.

24 3-OUNCE SERVINGS

FROM THE TROPICS

Exotic coolers from Cancer to Capricorn

DO YOU DREAM OF A FIJI IDYLL, OR OF QUAFFING A
FROSTY RUM-LACED SUNDOWNER IN OLD HAVANA?
TROPICAL QUENCHERS ARE DESIGNED FOR LANGUID
SIPPING, PREFERABLY UNDER A PALM TREE OR IN A
WHITEWASHED HOTEL WITH DISCREET SERVICE.
DON'T FORGET THE LITTLE PAPER UMBRELLAS!

BAHAMA MAMA

1/2 oz. 151-proof rum
1/2 oz. coconut rum or coconut liqueur
1/2 oz. dark rum
1/2 oz. coffee liqueur
4 oz. pineapple juice
Juice of 1/2 fresh lemon

Mix all ingredients in a cocktail shaker with cracked ice. Strain into an iced highball glass and garnish with fresh fruit.

BEACHCOMBER

1-1/2 oz. light rum
1/2 oz. Cointreau
1/2 oz. fresh lime juice
2 dashes maraschino liqueur or grenadine

Mix all ingredients with crushed ice in blender or mixer. Pour (don't strain) into wine goblet and garnish with a lime wheel.

BLUE HAWAIIAN

1 oz. light rum
1 oz. blue Curaçao
1 oz. cream of coconut
2 oz. pineapple juice

Mix all ingredients in a cocktail shaker with cracked ice. Strain into an iced highball glass and garnish with fresh fruit.

CUBA LIBRE

Although the Cuba Libre might be assigned to the Highball category (p. 29), the lure of the tropics is simply irresistible. The addition of fresh lime elevates it to the sublime.

2 oz. light rum
Juice and fruit of 1/2 lime
Cola

Squeeze lime and drop fruit into an iced highball glass. Add rum and fill with cola.

PAPA HEMINGWAY'S LEGACY

The DAIQUIRI was a favorite drink of one of the twentieth century's greatest drinking personalities, Ernest Hemingway, who lived in Cuba during Prohibition. He made the drink popular while waiting for literary inspiration in the bar of Havana's Hotel Floridita.

BASIC DAIQUIRI

1-1/2 oz. light rum
1 oz. fresh lime juice
1 tsp. sugar

Shake well with cracked ice and strain into a chilled cocktail glass. Garnish with a slice of lime or maraschino cherry. It would be sacrilegious to use Rose's lime juice in this drink.

FROZEN DAIQUIRI FOR TWO

3 oz. light rum
3 oz. frozen limeade concentrate
1 Tbs. triple sec
6-8 ice cubes

Place ingredients in blender and blend until slushy. Serve in iced cocktail glasses with lime slices or mint sprigs. For elegant presentation, moisten cocktail glass rims and spin in granulated sugar.

BANANA DAIQUIRI

1-1/2 oz. light rum
1/2 oz. lime juice
1/3 of a ripe banana
1 tsp. sugar or banana liqueur
3-4 ice cubes

Blend until slushy and pour into a frosted parfait glass. Garnish with a skewer of fresh fruit.

HEMINGWAY'S FLORIDITA DAIQUIRI

2 oz. light rum
2 oz. grapefruit juice
1 oz. fresh lime juice
1 oz. simple syrup

Mix all ingredients and serve frozen or over crushed ice in a chilled cocktail glass. Garnish with grapefruit slice.

Frozen Peach or Strawberry Daiquiri

1-1/2 oz. light rum
3/4 oz. Curaçao or triple sec
3/4 oz. lime juice
1/2 tsp. sugar
1/2 fresh peach (peeled) or 6 ripe strawberries, hulled
4-5 ice cubes

Blend and serve in a chilled wine glass. Garnish with a slice of fresh fruit.

Hurricane

1 oz. light rum
1 oz. dark rum
1/2 oz. passion fruit syrup
1/2 oz. fresh lime juice
1-1/2 oz. fresh orange juice
1-1/2 oz. pineapple juice
Dash of bitters

Mix in a cocktail shaker with cracked ice and strain into a chilled wine glass. Garnish with fresh fruit.

KAMIKAZE

The Kamikaze is popular as a "shooter"— served in a shot glass. Don't be fooled; purists will drink this as a proper cocktail.

1-1/2 oz. vodka
1 oz. triple sec
1 oz. fresh lime juice

Squeeze lime juice into a cocktail shaker. Add other ingredients, and shake with cracked ice. Strain into a chilled shot glass or cocktail glass.

TRADER VIC—THE GODFATHER OF TIKI

Victor Bergeron founded the legendary Trader Vic's restaurant (originally called "Hinky Dinks"), the original Polynesian-themed Tiki Bar. Tiki culture has since spread far and wide. Vic also invented the quintessential tropical cooler, the MAI TAI, in 1944.

MAI TAI

Trader Vic claimed that Mai Tai is a Tahitian phrase meaning, "out of this world" or "the best." Vic's 1944 original called for specialized and exotic ingredients, but the recipe has been simplified over the years.

2 oz. golden rum
1/2 oz. Curaçao
1/2 oz. orgeat (almond-flavored) syrup
1/4 oz. rock candy syrup or simple syrup
Juice of 1 fresh lime

Squeeze lime juice into a cocktail shaker. Add other ingredients and shake with cracked ice. Strain into a chilled old fashioned glass and garnish with mint sprigs.

MARGARITA

Almost as popular as the Martini, Miss Margarita has engendered countless variations, along with a specialized saucer-shaped vessel, the better to partake of her sweetly salty pleasures. Here is a sampling, along with the original recipe for the lady who caused all the fuss.

BASIC MARGARITA

1-1/2 oz. tequila
1/2 oz. triple sec
Juice of 1/2 fresh lemon or lime

Moisten the rim of a chilled cocktail glass or margarita glass with lemon or lime and dip glass rim in salt. Mix all ingredients in a cocktail shaker with cracked ice. Strain into salted glass. Garnish with a lemon or lime wedge.

BLUE MARGARITA

1-1/2 oz. tequila
1/2 oz. blue Curaçao
Juice of 1/2 fresh lemon or lime

Mix and serve as for BASIC MARGARITA.

CRANBERRY MARGARITAS BY THE PITCHER

1 cup tequila
1/3 cup triple sec
3/4 cup fresh lime juice
1-1/4 cups cranberry juice
1-1/2 cup frozen cranberries, rinsed
1/3-1/2 cup sugar

Mix all ingredients in a large measuring cup or bowl. Pour half of mixture into blender and fill blender with ice. Blend until slushy. Repeat with rest of mixture. Serve with fresh lime wedges.

FROZEN MARGARITA

Place Basic Margarita ingredients in blender with 4-5 ice cubes and blend until slushy. Frost the rim of a parfait glass with salt (see above). Pour mixture into salted parfait glass.

STRAWBERRY MARGARITA

1 oz. tequila
1/2 oz. triple sec
1/2 oz. strawberry liqueur
Juice of 1/2 fresh lemon or lime
1 oz. frozen strawberries

Moisten the rim of a chilled cocktail glass or margarita glass with lemon or lime and dip glass rim in salt. Mix all ingredients in a cocktail shaker with cracked ice. Strain into salted glass. Garnish with a lemon or lime wedge. For a frozen version, blend with 4-5 cubes of cracked ice and pour into salted parfait glass. Garnish with a fresh strawberry or lime wedge.

MELON BALL

3/4 oz. vodka
3/4 oz. Midori or melon liqueur
5 oz. orange juice or pineapple juice

Mix ingredients in a cocktail shaker and strain into an iced highball glass. Garnish with an orange wheel or a slice of melon.

MINT JULEP

Favored by antebellum planters, juleps date to the 1660s (Samuel Pepys mentions juleps). Don't be seen at the Kentucky Derby without one!

4 oz. bourbon
1 tsp. simple syrup
Fresh mint sprigs

Muddle 4 mint sprigs and simple syrup in the bottom of a chilled highball glass. Fill glass with crushed ice; then add bourbon. Stir until glass is frosted. Garnish with 4 more sprigs of fresh mint and fresh fruit, and serve with straws.

MINT JULEP, SOUTHERN STYLE

Fill a chilled highball glass with crushed ice and add 4 ounces bourbon. Without touching the glass, stir until the glass is frosted. Add 1 teaspoon simple syrup and fill with water or soda water. Add sprigs of fresh mint so that tops extend 2 inches above the rim of the glass. Serve with short straws so that the drinker buries his nose in the mint while drinking and inhales the fragrance.

MOJITO

1-1/2 oz. light rum
1 tsp. simple syrup
Juice of 1 fresh lime
Soda water
Mint leaves

Muddle mint leaves with simple syrup in a chilled old fashioned glass. Add cracked ice, lime juice, and rum. Fill with soda water and garnish with more fresh mint leaves.

PIMM'S CUP

First served as a digestive tonic in James Pimm's London oyster bar during the 1880s, the refreshing Pimm's Cup is the beverage of choice for devotees of 5-day cricket matches.

2 oz. Pimm's No. 1
4 oz. ginger ale or lemon-lime soda

Pour Pimm's into an iced highball glass and fill with ginger ale or lemon-lime soda. Garnish with a slice of cucumber.

PIÑA COLADA

Although they're the gaudy, overdressed party girls of the cocktail world, you can't help loving piña coladas—they're so sweet and tasty.

1-1/2 oz. golden rum
1-1/2 oz. coconut cream
4 oz. pineapple juice
4-5 ice cubes

Blend all ingredients in blender until slushy. Pour into a chilled parfait glass or half coconut shell and garnish with pineapple chunks and a cherry.

YELLOW BIRD

1-1/2 oz. light rum
1/2 oz. Galliano
1/2 oz. triple sec or Curaçao
1/2 oz. fresh lime juice

Mix ingredients in a cocktail shaker and strain into a chilled cocktail glass. Garnish with an orange or lime wheel.

ZOMBIE

1-1/2 oz. dark rum
3/4 oz. golden rum
3/4 oz. light rum
1/2 oz. apricot brandy
1/2 oz. 151-proof Demerara rum
1 oz. unsweetened pineapple juice
3/4 oz. papaya or passion fruit juice
Juice of 1 fresh lime

Mix all ingredients in a cocktail shaker with cracked ice and strain into an iced highball glass. Float Demerara rum on top and garnish with a mint sprig dusted with powdered sugar.

NAUGHTY DRINKS

With names to make your mother blush!

ARE YOU BOLD ENOUGH TO ASK FOR ONE OF THESE
RACY COCKTAILS? THEY MAY HAVE NAUGHTY-SOUNDING
NAMES, BUT THEY'RE OH-SO-NICE! WE SUGGEST
SLIPPING INTO SOMETHING MORE COMFORTABLE . . .

BETWEEN THE SHEETS

3/4 oz. cognac
3/4 oz. Cointreau
3/4 oz. rum
Juice of 2 fresh lemons

Mix with cracked ice and strain into a chilled cocktail glass. Garnish with a twist of lemon peel.

FRENCH KISS

1/2 oz. Amaretto
1/2 oz. crème de cacao
1/2 oz. Irish Cream liqueur

Carefully layer all ingredients into a shot glass.

HOT PANTS

1-1/2 oz. tequila
3/4 oz. peppermint schnapps
3/4 oz. grapefruit juice
Dash of grenadine—to taste

Moisten the rim of a chilled cocktail glass with a little grapefruit juice. Lightly frost the rim of the glass with sugar. Mix ingredients with cracked ice and strain into glass.

NAKED LADY

1-1/2 oz. light rum
1/2 oz. pineapple juice
1/2 oz. apricot brandy

Shake well with cracked ice and strain into a chilled cocktail glass. Garnish with pineapple and cherry.

ORGASM

1/2 oz. Irish cream liqueur
1/2 oz. peppermint schnapps

Serve in a shot glass.

QUICKIE

1 oz. bourbon
1 oz. light rum
1/4 oz. triple sec

Mix with cracked ice and strain into a chilled cocktail glass. Garnish with a twist of orange peel or orange slice.

SEX ON THE BEACH

1 oz. vodka

3 oz. cranberry juice

3 oz. orange or pineapple juice

1 oz. peach schnapps

Pour ingredients into an iced highball glass, and stir.

SILK PANTIES

1-1/2 oz. vodka

1/2 oz. peach schnapps

Mix ingredients with cracked ice, and strain into a chilled shot glass.

SKINNY DIPPER

2 oz. melon liqueur
6 oz. cranberry juice

Serve over ice in a tall glass.

SLOW COMFORTABLE SCREW

1 oz. vodka
3/4 oz. Southern Comfort
3/4 oz. sloe gin
4 oz. fresh orange juice

Shake well with cracked ice and strain into an iced highball glass. Garnish with an orange slice.

FINISHING TOUCHES

Drinks... dessert... or both?

THEIR POTENCY DISGUISED WITH CREAM, SWEET
DESSERT DRINKS HAVE LONG BEEN CONSIDERED THE
PURVIEW OF TIMID DRINKERS. NOT SO! AN ELEGANT
NIGHTCAP CAN ADD JUST THE RIGHT TOUCH OF
SWEETNESS AS YOU WIND DOWN THE EVENING
WITH A SPECIAL SOMEONE.

ALEXANDER

Here is the original, followed by its more popular variation.

1 oz. gin
1 oz. crème de cacao
1 oz. heavy cream

Shake gently with cracked ice and strain into a chilled cocktail glass. Garnish with freshly grated nutmeg.

BRANDY ALEXANDER

Substitute 1 oz. brandy for gin.

ANGEL'S KISS

Here's a classic example of a Pousse Café. Pour ingredients with great care and in the order listed here so that they float atop one another and do not mix.

1/4 oz. crème de cacao
1/4 oz. crème d'Yvette
1/4 oz. brandy
1/4 oz. heavy cream

Place a spoon, round side up, into the Pousse Café glass and pour the liquid slowly over the back of the spoon. Use a different spoon for each ingredient, and don't allow the spoon to touch the liquid already in the glass.

ANGEL'S TIP

3/4 oz. crème de cacao
1/4 oz. heavy cream

Float cream on top of crème de cacao. Top with a cherry.

B-52

1/3 oz. Kahlúa
1/3 oz. Irish cream liqueur
1/3 oz. Grand Marnier

Float ingredients in a pousse café glass as listed.

BLACK RUSSIAN

1-1/2 oz. vodka
3/4 oz. Kahlúa

Shake well with cracked ice and strain into a chilled old fashioned glass. May also be served on the rocks.

Add a few drops of fresh lemon juice, and—presto—a BLACK MAGIC.

DEATH BY CHOCOLATE

3/4 oz. vodka
3/4 oz. dark crème de cacao
3/4 oz. Irish cream liqueur
1 scoop chocolate ice cream

Blend all ingredients with crushed ice and pour into a chilled parfait glass. Garnish with shaved chocolate and a dollop of whipped cream.

GOLDEN CADILLAC

1-1/2 oz. white crème de cacao
3/4 oz. Galliano
1-1/2 oz. heavy cream

Shake well with cracked ice and strain into a chilled cocktail glass.

GRASSHOPPER

3/4 oz. green crème de menthe
3/4 oz. crème de cacao
3/4 oz. heavy cream

Shake well with cracked ice and strain into a chilled cocktail glass. Although not traditional, mint sprigs would be a nice touch.

IRISH COFFEE

1-1/2 oz. Irish or blended whiskey
1-1/2 tsp. sugar (to taste)
4 oz. hot, strong, black coffee

Mix coffee and sugar in an Irish coffee glass or mug. Add whiskey and top with whipped cream. Garnish with a sprinkle of cinnamon or chocolate curls.

As variations, substitute Kahlúa, Tia Maria, or other liqueur of your choice for the whiskey.

MUDSLIDE

3/4 oz. vodka
3/4 oz. Kahlúa
3/4 oz. Irish cream liqueur

Shake all ingredients with cracked ice and strain into a chilled cocktail glass. Garnish with chocolate curls or cocoa powder.

To serve frozen: blend all ingredients with crushed ice and pour into a chilled parfait glass.

PARISIAN BLOND COCKTAIL

We don't know whether you will feel like a Parisian blonde after drinking one of these, but the editors would love to hear from Parisian blondes—whether or not they've sampled this cocktail.

3/4 oz. Jamaica rum
3/4 oz. light rum
3/4 oz. Cointreau

Shake all ingredients with cracked ice and strain into a chilled cocktail glass. Garnish with a twist of orange peel.

PINK LADY

Robust shaking is the key to preparing this frothy little lady.

1-1/2 oz. gin
1 tsp. grenadine
1 tsp. heavy cream
1 egg white (or 3 Tbs. pasteurized egg white substitute)

Shake vigorously with cracked ice and strain into a chilled cocktail glass.

PINK SQUIRREL

The delicate almond flavor of this cocktail comes from the addition of crème de noyaux— made from the pits of peaches and apricots. Many people go "nuts" for this classic.

3/4 oz. white crème de cacao
3/4 oz. crème de noyaux
3/4 oz. heavy cream

Shake ingredients with cracked ice and strain into a chilled cocktail glass.

SILK STOCKING

1 oz. tequila
1/2 oz. white crème de cacao
1/2 oz. Chambord
1/2 oz. heavy cream

Shake ingredients with cracked ice and strain into a chilled cocktail glass.

WHITE RUSSIAN

1 oz. vodka
1 oz. Kahlúa
1 oz. heavy cream

Shake ingredients with cracked ice and strain into an iced old fashioned glass.

How to Cure a Hangover

The only true cure for a hangover is time—24 hours, to be exact—but in the interim, some of the following may provide relief. And we would never say "we told you so."

- Don't overindulge to begin with. (OK, we told you so.)
- Drink lots of water, cola, or fruit juice.
- Sleep.
- Nibble on foods high in B vitamins.
- Try a spicy VIRGIN MARY.
- Refrain from "hair of the dog," no matter how tempting.

KNOW YOUR SPIRITS

Glossary

THE MORE YOU KNOW, THE MORE FUN YOU CAN HAVE.

ONCE YOU MASTER THE BASICS, YOU CAN

DAZZLE YOUR FRIENDS WITH YOUR EXPERTISE

AND BECOME A TRUE BON VIVEUR.

ABSINTHE

An anise-flavored drink made from worm-wood. Although popular during the 19th century, it is no longer available in the U.S. because of the toxic effects of the wormwood.

AMARETTO

Almond-flavored liqueur made from apricot pits.

AMER PICON

Orange-flavored French liqueur made from spices and quinine. Has a bitter taste.

APERITIF

A cocktail or other drink taken before a meal to stimulate the appetite.

ARMAGNAC

French brandy distilled from grapes and produced only in the Armagnac region of France. Has a delicate, dry taste.

BENEDICTINE

Herb liqueur produced by Benedictine

monks using a secret recipe.

BITTERS

Made from roots, berries, herbs, and bark, bitters are always characterized by their bitter, aromatic flavor. The best-known is ANGOSTURA BITTERS, made in Trinidad. PEYCHAUD'S BITTERS—made in New Orleans, naturally—is a crucial ingredient in a SAZERAC COCKTAIL. A few drops are all you'll ever need.

BLENDED WHISKEY
See Whiskey.

BOURBON
See Whiskey.

BRANDY

Generic term for distilled spirits made from grapes. Brandy can be flavored with many different types of fruit.

CACHAÇA

Produced in Brazil, this colorless spirit is

distilled from sugar cane.

CHAMBORD
Produced in France, this liqueur is made from cognac and an infusion of small black raspberries. It also contains the flavors of currant, blackberries, and red raspberries.

CHAMPAGNE
A refined sparkling wine, produced in the Champagne region of France. Only champagne made in Champagne may be so named. Other sparkling wines may be designated "méthode champenoise," meaning that they were produced following the method used in Champagne.

CHARTREUSE
Green and yellow herbal liqueurs distilled from more than 130 plants by Carthusian monks.

CHERRY HEERING
A Danish liqueur that is deep red and flavored with black cherries. Unlike many fruit

liqueurs, it is not overly sweet.

COGNAC
Aromatic, smooth brandy produced only in the Cognac region of France.

COINTREAU
This crystal-clear liqueur blends the flavors of sweet and bitter oranges.

CORDIAL
See Liqueur.

CORDIAL MÉDOC
A red fruit liqueur made with red Bordeaux wine.

CRÈME
These cordials all have a high sugar content:

CRÈME DE CACAO
Available in white and dark varieties, it is made from cacao and vanilla beans.
CRÈME DE CASSIS
Flavored with blackcurrants.

CRÈME DE MENTHE
Mint-flavored liqueur available in green and white varieties.

CRÈME NOYAUX
Made from peach and apricot pits, with a subtle almond flavor.

CRÈME D'YVETTE
Violet-flavored.

CURAÇAO
Liqueur produced in the Dutch West Indies and flavored with dried orange peel. Available in white and blue, it's a crucial ingredient in many blue cocktails.

DRAMBUIE
From the Gaelic *an dram buidheach* (the drink that satisfies), this liqueur from the Scottish Isle of Skye is a blend of Scotch whisky, honey, and herbs.

DRY
In cocktail terms, dry means "not sweet." Dryness results during fermentation as sugar

is converted to alcohol.

FLIP

A type of cocktail made with liquor, sugar, and a raw egg, and sometimes with cream. For safety, substitute pasteurized for raw eggs.

FIZZES

Cousins of Collins, they contain liquor, citrus juices, and sugar. Ingredients are shaken vigorously and poured into iced old fashioned glasses and topped with carbonated mixers.

FRANGELICO

The 300-year-old recipe for this Italian liqueur includes hazelnuts and an infusion of berries and flowers.

GALLIANO

An Italian liqueur, yellow in color, flavored with herbs, flowers and spices, including anise, licorice and vanilla.

GIN

A colorless spirit distilled from grain and

flavored with juniper berries. Nowadays, when people refer to gin, they usually mean LONDON DRY GIN—lacking in sweetness and most often used in cocktails. HOLLAND GIN is highly aromatic and flavorful. OLD TOM GIN has been sweetened with sugar syrup.

GRAND MARNIER
Created in 1880, this French liqueur is made from cognac, the essence of wild oranges, and other ingredients whose identity is a closely-guarded secret.

GRENADINE
A sweet liqueur made from pomegranates. Often used for its crimson color.

IRISH CREAM
This liqueur is made from a pasteurized mix of cream, eggs, chocolate, and Irish whiskey. Store opened bottles in the refrigerator.

IRISH WHISKEY
Irish whiskey is made from a blend of fer-

mented grain and malted barley, and produced only in Ireland.

KAHLÚA

From Mexico, this sweet liqueur features the flavors of coffee and vanilla.

KÜMMEL

An herbal liqueur made from anise and caraway seeds.

LILLET

A French aperitif wine, similar to vermouth.

LIQUEUR

Liqueurs and cordials are the same. Often sweet and brightly colored, they are made by distilling neutral spirits with fruit, flowers, and/or herbs. Liqueurs have strong flavors and should be used sparingly.

MARASCHINO

Refers to a type of cherry grown in Dalmatia, and the liqueur distilled therefrom.

MIDORI

A brand of green melon-flavored liqueur.

MUDDLE

To mash fruit, herbs, and/or sugar in the bottom of the glass to release their flavors. A muddler is a small wooden or glass pestle.

NEUTRAL SPIRITS

These are distilled from grain and produce a practically tasteless, colorless alcohol that is the basis for many other spirits and liqueurs.

ORGEAT

Syrup made from almonds, sugar, and rose water or orange-flower water. The flavor of almonds dominates. Because orgeat is difficult to obtain, almond syrup may be substituted.

PARFAIT D'AMOUR

This violet liqueur has a delicate flavor of rose petals and orange, with a hint of vanilla. It is made with orange peel, vanilla pods, almonds, and rose petals.

PERNOD

Clear yellow-green in the bottle, this anise-flavored aperitif is often used as an absinthe substitute, and will turn cloudy-white when mixed with water or ice.

PIMM'S

A brand of liqueurs made in England using a secret recipe including herbs and quinine. The best known of these—and what people are referring to when they order a PIMM'S CUP—is Pimm's No. 1, which has a gin base.

PROOF

Measures alcoholic strength or content of a particular spirit. One degree of proof equals one half of one percent of alcohol. Therefore, a spirit labeled "80 proof" contains 40 percent alcohol.

RICKEY

A type of cocktail prepared with liquor, lime juice, and soda water served on the rocks in an old fashioned glass.

RUM

Distilled from the fermented juice of sugar cane and molasses, rum is produced in the world's tropical regions. Rums vary by color, weight, and sweetness. More molasses produces a darker, sweeter rum. A light rum has very little molasses taste, and will be drier.

SAKE

This Japanese wine is made from rice and traditionally served warm in small porcelain cups.

SAMBUCA

A liqueur produced by the infusion of witch elder and licorice. The licorice flavor predominates. It is similar to Anisette but has a higher alcoholic level and is less sugary. Available in white (clear) and black varieties.

SCHNAPPS

Stronger and less sweet than liqueurs, schnapps are usually made from neutral spirits and flavored with fruit or peppermint.

SCOTCH WHISKY

Note the absence of the "e." The term "whisky" derives originally from the Gaelic *uisge beatha*, meaning "water of life." Scotch whisky is produced only in Scotland, from malted barley. Its characteristic smoky flavor is produced when the malted barley is dried over peat fires. Purists eschew blends—the inclusion of spirits distilled from grains other than barley—in favor of the SINGLE MALT (all-barley) variety.

SLINGS

Fruity Asian imports redolent of languid tropical hotels, Slings contain liquor (usually gin), fruit brandy, a carbonated mixer, and sometimes fruit juice and a spiral fruit peel garnish.

SLOE GIN

Not gin at all, but a liqueur made from sloe berries.

SMASHES

Liquor of choice and simple syrup served in an iced old fashioned glass with sprigs of mint and fruit. OLD FASHIONED meets MINT JULEP.

SOUTHERN COMFORT

First produced in New Orleans in 1874, this liqueur has a bourbon base and is flavored with peach.

TEQUILA

Colorless Mexican liquor made from the mescal plant.

TIA MARIA

This coffee-flavored liqueur from Jamaica has a rum base.

TRIPLE SEC

Liqueur similar to Curaçao, but less sweet.

VERMOUTH

An aperitif wine flavored with herbs, roots, berries, flowers, and seeds. French (dry) vermouth, has a delicate, slightly nutty flavor, and is pale gold in color. Italian (sweet) vermouth has a darker color and a sweeter flavor.

VODKA

A colorless spirit, historically made with potatoes. Vodka produced in the U.S. is distilled from grain and filtered through activated charcoal. Flavored vodkas include lemon, blackcurrant, apple, and vanilla.

WHISKEY

All whiskey is made from fermented grain mash. The type of grain used will determine the taste and type of whiskey. The mash is aged in oak barrels, which produces its distinctive color, aroma, and taste.

BLENDED WHISKEY

Made with several types of grain including corn, rye, and barley, mixed with neutral grain spirits.

BOURBON WHISKEY

First produced in Bourbon County,

Kentucky. For a whiskey to be called "Bourbon," the main ingredient must be corn. The whiskey must age for four years in oak, and never be blended with neutral grain spirits. It has a smooth, full flavor.

RYE WHISKEY
The main ingredient is rye, mixed with other neutral spirits. Rye produces a heavier-bodied whiskey.

IRISH WHISKEY, SCOTCH WHISKY
See individual entries.

INDEX

151

DRINKS BY PRIMARY ALCOHOLIC INGREDIENT

Blended Whiskey/Rye

DRINKS BY COLOR/FLAVORING

Anise-Flavored Drinks

Apricot/Peach Drinks

Berry Drinks

Blue and Purple Drinks